GRAPHIC LIBRARY®

GRAPHIC SCIENCE

INVESTIGATING THE

SCIENTIFIC METHOD

WITH

SUPER SCIENTIST

by Donald B. Lemke

illustrated by Tod Smith and Al Milgrom

Consultant:
Leslie Flynn, PhD
Science Education, Chemistry
University of Minnesota

Capstone press®

Mankato, Minnesota

Graphic Library is published by Capstone Press,
151 Good Counsel Drive, P.O. Box 669, Mankato, Minnesota 5
www.capstonepress.com

1 2 3 4 5 6 13 12 11 10 09 08

Library of Congress Cataloging-in-Publication Data
Lemke, Donald B.
  Investigating the scientific method with Max Axiom, super scientist / by Donald B.
Lemke; illustrated by Tod Smith and Al Milgrom.
    p. cm. — (Graphic library. Graphic science)
  Summary: "In graphic novel format, follows the adventures of Max Axiom as he
explains the scientific method" — Provided by publisher.
  Includes bibliographical references and index.
  ISBN-13: 978-1-4296-1329-3 (hardcover)
  ISBN-10: 1-4296-1329-7 (hardcover)
  ISBN-13: 978-1-4296-1760-4 (softcover pbk.)
  ISBN-10: 1-4296-1760-8 (softcover pbk.)
  1. Science — Methodology — Juvenile literature. I. Smith, Tod, ill. II. Milgrom, Al, ill.
III. Title. IV. Series.
Q175.2.L46 2008
507.2 — dc22   2007022792

Art Director and Designer
Bob Lentz

Cover Artist
Tod Smith

Colorist
Krista Ward

Editor
Christopher L. Harbo

Photo illustration credits: Alamy/Visual & Written SL, 15

TABLE OF CONTENTS

Sounds like a big problem.

Luckily, scientists have a process for solving problems and answering questions. This process is known as the scientific method and often has a few basic steps.

Steps of the Scientific Method
• Ask a question
• Gather information
• Form a hypothesis
• Design an experiment
• Collect data
• Analyze data and draw conclusions
• Communicate results

The order or number of these steps can always change, but scientists often rely on these basic methods to organize information.

DEFINITION

levee (LEV-ee)
a bank built up near a
river to prevent flooding

Come on. I'll take you through the scientific way to find answers.

First, choose a topic that interests you.

Scientists work in many fields. Plants, weather, animals, and even video games are great science topics to investigate.

After choosing a topic, form a question. Questions that can be answered "yes" or "no" don't require much research.

YES-OR-NO QUESTION: Do most birds fly?

OPEN-ENDED QUESTION: Why do birds fly south for the winter?

Instead, form open-ended questions that can be answered with a thoughtful statement.

Also, consider the amount of time available and the cost involved. Studying the effects of acid rain on a copper fountain could take weeks.

Instead, start with the question, "How does lemon juice affect this copper penny?" The results might surprise you.

The information you gather may show the question has already been answered. Don't worry. The experiment can still teach you a lot about the process of science.

And repeating the original research can never hurt. Thanks, Mrs. Vargas!

The library offers a great foundation of information, and experts can help build on that knowledge.

Teachers, engineers, or other scientists can provide details not available in books or on the Web.

THE INTERNET

ACCESS GRANTED: MAX AXIOM

With more than 100 million web sites, the Internet is an information gold mine. But even gold miners dig through a lot of rubble to find a shiny nugget. Fortunately, one word can guide anyone toward the riches of the Internet.

Note the date: Is the information current?

Evaluate the source: Is the Web site reliable?

Track the information: Does the Web site say where the information came from?

Sounds complicated. A detailed procedure must be useful in your work.

Oh, yes. I know the variables. Now, I'm writing a plan, which includes a materials list, dates and times, and exact instructions.

This information, along with any diagrams, will help guide me through the project.

It will also help others reproduce the experiment in the future.

Thanks for the tour of Aquarius, Amar! But I better get going before the city is underwater as well.

MORE ABOUT AQUARIUS

ACCESS GRANTED: MAX AXIOM

Aquarius is located 63 feet (19 meters) beneath the ocean surface in the Florida Keys National Marine Sanctuary. *Aquarius* allows scientists to stay underwater for an extended period of time. The extra time allows longer research, including coral reef monitoring and NASA equipment testing.

Wow! The soil is quickly crumbling, but the clay levee still holds. The rocks are strong too, but water easily leaks through the cracks.

Measure the dependent variable of water leaking through the levees. Also, record other observations by taking notes, keeping a journal, and even snapping a few pictures . . .

Oops! Sorry, mini mayor.

ROCK

BUILD A LEVEE

So, you want to build a levee like Max Axiom? Follow these simple instructions:

What you need:
- Ruler
- Plastic container
- Waterproof marker
- Sand, rocks, or clay
- Water
- Paper and pencil

What you do:
- Using the ruler, measure the depth of the plastic container.
- With the waterproof marker, write depth marks every 1/2 inch (1.3 centimeters) on the side of the container.
- Using the sand, clay, or rocks, build a wall dividing the inside of the container in half.
- Fill one side of the container with a desired amount of water.
- After one minute, record how much has drained to the other side.
- Repeat the experiment with a different material.

The information gathered is known as data. Scientists use data to draw conclusions about an experiment.

But piles and piles of raw data are nearly as useless as no data at all.

Raw data needs to be analyzed to make the information helpful.

Charts and graphs are great tools for completing this step of the scientific method.

Line graphs show the interaction between two pieces of information.

ROCK
SOIL
CLAY

Water (gallons)

Time (minutes)

This line graph explains the water lost through each levee over time.

The clock is ticking, and the mayor expects results soon.

But analyzing the information isn't enough. Scientists study the trends of their data to develop a final conclusion.

A conclusion explains whether or not the original hypothesis was correct. In this case, the data clearly shows that clay allows the least amount of water to escape. The original hypothesis was correct!

Sometimes a hypothesis is false. Even a false hypothesis can teach scientists about what works and what doesn't.

Either way, the conclusion to a science experiment should be recorded.

The clay levee held back more water than rock or soil.

MORE ABOUT THE SCIENTIFIC METHOD

Throughout history, people have answered questions by observing and recording data. No one knows who developed the scientific method. Still, many believe Francesco Redi, an Italian physician, performed the first experiment to match this step-by-step plan. In 1668, most scientists believed maggots grew directly from rotten meat. Redi, however, believed maggots hatched from fly eggs. He proved this idea correct by forming a hypothesis, designing an experiment, and analyzing the data.

Scientists work in many fields and don't always answer their questions in the same way. An astronomer will investigate questions about the design of the universe in a way that will differ from a chemist trying to discover the structure of matter. Some scientists conduct experimental studies while others rely on observations and interviews. The methods scientists use to gather data depend on the questions they are trying to answer.

With more than 130 million items, the Library of Congress in Washington, D.C., is the largest library in the world. Instead of strolling through the library's 530 miles (853 kilometers) of bookshelves, researchers often browse materials on their own computer. Like many libraries today, many of the Library of Congress' resources are available on the Internet.

Scientists often test large experiments on miniature models. In the early 1900s, inventors Wilbur and Orville Wright tested more than 200 miniature airplane wings inside their 16-inch (41-centimeter) wide wind tunnel. After finding the best design, the inventors built full-size versions of the wings. On December 17, 1903, their wings made history as part of the first powered airplane to take flight.

Each year, hundreds of young scientists compete at the International Science and Engineering Fair (ISEF). As the largest science competition for students, ISEF judges must choose from the best science projects in the world. In 2006, they awarded $4 million in scholarships and prizes to the top competitors.

Aquanauts experiment inside *Aquarius*, but scientists studying space head to the *International Space Station*. This giant series of modules orbits 250 miles (400 kilometers) above the earth. Scientists from around the globe, including U.S. astronauts, use the station as a laboratory and observatory.

MORE ABOUT

MAX AXIOM
SUPER SCIENTIST

Real name: Maxwell J. Axiom
Hometown: Seattle, Washington
Height: 6' 1" **Weight:** 192 lbs
Eyes: Brown **Hair:** None

Super capabilities: Super intelligence; able to shrink to the size of an atom; sunglasses give x-ray vision; lab coat allows for travel through time and space.

Origin: Since birth, Max Axiom seemed destined for greatness. His mother, a marine biologist, taught her son about the mysteries of the sea. His father, a nuclear physicist and volunteer park ranger, schooled Max on the wonders of earth and sky.

One day on a wilderness hike, a megacharged lightning bolt struck Max with blinding fury. When he awoke, Max discovered a newfound energy and set out to learn as much about science as possible. He traveled the globe earning degrees in every aspect of the field. Upon his return, he was ready to share his knowledge and new identity with the world. He had become Max Axiom, Super Scientist.

GLOSSARY

analyze (AN-uh-lize) — to examine something carefully in order to understand it

aquanaut (AK-wuh-nawt) — a scuba diver who lives and works inside and outside an underwater shelter for an extended period

conclusion (kuhn-KLOO-shuhn) — a decision or realization based on the facts available

controlled variable (kuhn-TROHLD VAIR-ee-uh-buhl) — a part of an experiment that stays the same

data (DAY-tuh) — information or facts

dependent variable (dee-PEN-duhnt VAIR-ee-uh-buhl) — a measured result of a change in the independent variable of an experiment

evidence (EV-uh-duhnss) — information, items, and facts that help prove something is true or false

hypothesis (hye-POTH-uh-siss) — a prediction that can be tested about how a scientific investigation or experiment will turn out

independent variable (in-di-PEN-duhnt VAIR-ee-uh-buhl) — a part of an experiment that changes

observation (ob-zur-VAY-shuhn) — something that you have noticed by watching carefully

prediction (pri-DIK-shuhn) — a statement of what you think will happen in the future; a hypothesis is a scientific prediction.

procedure (pruh-SEE-jur) — a set way of doing something

research (REE-surch) — to study and learn about a subject

READ MORE

Bardhan-Quallen, Sudipta. *Last-Minute Science Fair Projects: When Your Bunsen's Not Burning but the Clock's Really Ticking.* New York: Sterling, 2006.

Carey, Stephen S. *A Beginner's Guide to Scientific Method.* Belmont, Calif.: Thomson/Wadsworth, 2004.

Harris, Elizabeth Snoke. *First Place Science Fair Projects for Inquisitive Kids.* New York: Lark Books, 2005.

Jerome, Kate Boehm. *Thinking It Through.* Math Behind the Science. Washington, D.C.: National Geographic Society, 2004.

Rosinsky, Natalie M. *How Scientists Work.* Simply Science. Minneapolis: Compass Point Books, 2004.

INTERNET SITES

FactHound offers a safe, fun way to find Internet sites related to this book. All of the sites on FactHound have been researched by our staff.

Here's how:
1. Visit *www.facthound.com*
2. Choose your grade level.
3. Type in this book ID **1429613297** for age-appropriate sites. You may also browse subjects by clicking on letters, or by clicking on pictures and words.
4. Click on the **Fetch It** button.

FactHound will fetch the best sites for you!

INDEX